Algeria, Morocco, Saudi Arabia:
Response to Terrorism

Algeria, Morocco, Saudi Arabia: Response to Terrorism

September 2015

Algeria, Morocco, and Saudi Arabia:
Responses to Terrorism

SUMMARY   Acts of terrorism committed on September 11, 2001, and subsequent international actions caused many countries, including Algeria, Morocco, and Saudi Arabia, to enhance their counterterrorism policies through amending existing or enacting new laws related to the criminal justice system. All three countries have adopted broad definitions of terrorism, raising concerns that they could include acts of political dissent within the ambit of acts of terrorism. At various points they have also adopted criminal procedure provisions that lowered certain restrictions for investigations of crimes labeled as crimes of terrorism, made the financing of terrorism a separate offense, and required all suspicious financial transactions to be subject to scrutiny by special financial units before they are referred to the competent criminal authorities. In addition, Morocco and Saudi Arabia recognize that there is a religious component to the acts of terrorism committed by many terrorist organizations. They proclaim to have established special programs to seek to address this element of terrorism by means other than the criminal justice system.

I. Introduction

Following the September 11, 2001, attacks (9/11 attacks) perpetrated against the United States by al-Qaeda claiming to act in accordance with Islamic religious teachings and beliefs, many countries adopted or enhanced the already existing measures relating to combatting terrorism.

On September 28, 2001, shortly after the 9/11 attacks, the UN Security Council approved Resolution 1373[1] under chapter VII of the Charter of the United Nations. This Resolution sets up a general framework to combat terrorism, concentrating mainly on how to prevent and suppress the financing of terrorism and on changing governmental attitudes and behaviors towards the growing threat of terrorism.

This report provides information about the counterterrorism measures adopted by three countries of the Middle East and North Africa region whose populations are either entirely or nearly all Muslims: Saudi Arabia, Algeria, and Morocco.

---

[1] S.C. Res. 1373, U.N. Doc. S/RES/1373 (Sept. 28, 2001), http://www.un.org/en/sc/ctc/specialmeetings/2012/docs/United%20Nations%20Security%20Council%20Resolution%201373%20%282001%29.pdf.

II. "Terrorism" Defined

UN Security Council Resolution 1373 calls on and requires all Member States to take necessary measures aimed at

- Preventing and suppressing the financing of terrorist activities by criminalizing all acts tending to provide for or facilitate such financing;

- Refraining from providing any assistance or support, passive or active, to persons or entities involved in terrorist activities; and

- Enhancing cooperation among states through the exchange of information and other measures to control and impede the movement of terrorists across international boundaries.

This Resolution does not provide a definition of what constitutes an act of terrorism, apparently leaving this task to each country to decide on its own. For example, United States federal law defines "terrorism" as any crime that appears to be intended to "intimidate or coerce a civilian population; to influence the policy of a government by intimidation or coercion; or to affect the conduct of a government by mass destruction, assassination, or kidnapping."[2] In October 2012, UN delegates from various countries called for increased international cooperation to "define terrorism and conclude a convention on the topic."[3]

In Algeria, article 87bis of the Algerian Penal Code defines a "terrorist act" as any act targeting state security and national unity, territorial integrity, and the stability and normal functioning of institutions by any action whose objective is to

- Spread terror among the population and create a climate of insecurity through moral or physical assault on people, through exposing their lives, freedom, or security to danger, or through damaging their properties;

- Obstruct traffic or freedom of movement on the roads and gather or sit in in public spaces;

- Assault the symbols of the Nation and the Republic and unearth or desecrate graves;

- Assault the means of transportation and transport, the public and private properties, and possess or occupy them without legal justification;

- Assault the environment or introduce into the atmosphere, into the earth or on its face, or into the waters, including territorial waters, a substance that would expose the health of humans or of animals, or the natural environment to danger;

- Obstruct the work of public authorities, the freedom of worship, the exercise of public liberties, or the functioning of the establishments assisting public services;

---

[2] 18 U.S.C. § 2331, http://www.law.cornell.edu/uscode/text/18/2331. *See also Definitions of Terrorism in the U.S. Code*, FEDERAL BUREAU OF INVESTIGATION, http://www.fbi.gov/about-us/investigate/terrorism/terrorism-definition (last visited Sept. 18, 2014).
[3] Press Release, U.N. General Assembly, Legal Committee Urges Conclusion of Draft Comprehensive Convention on International Terrorism, GA/L/3433 (Oct. 8, 2012), http://www.un.org/News/Press/docs/2012/gal3433.doc htm.

- Obstruct the functioning of public institutions, assault the lives or properties of their representatives, or impede the implementation of laws and regulations.[4]

In Morocco, the determining factor in the definition of a "terrorist act" is whether there is an intention to seriously undermine public order. Article 218bis of the Penal Code stipulates that

> [t]he following crimes shall constitute terrorist acts if they are intentionally related to individual or collective enterprise having the objective of gravely undermining the public order through intimidation, terror, or violence.[5]

In Saudi Arabia, article 1(a) of the Law Concerning Offenses of Terrorism and its Financing, issued on December 27, 2013, defines a terrorist crime as

> [a]ny act undertaken by the offender directly or indirectly in pursuance of an individual or collective criminal enterprise intended to disturb the public order, destabilize the security of society or the stability of the state, expose its national unity to danger, obstruct the implementation of the organic law or some of its provisions, harm the reputation of the state or its standing, endanger any of the state facilities or its natural resources, force any of its authorities to do or abstain from doing something, or threaten to carry out actions leading to any of the aforementioned objectives or encourage their accomplishment.[6]

The above definitions in the laws of Saudi Arabia, Algeria, and Morocco, while different, may each be seen as being so broad as to possibly include in the definition of terrorism all activities targeting a government or the political regime, even when such activities may involve legitimate political dissent or protest.[7] For example, a July 2014 article by Amnesty International reports that the Specialized Criminal Court in Jeddah "invoked article 21 of Saudi Arabia's repressive new anti-terrorism law" to convict and sentence a prominent Saudi Arabian lawyer and human rights defender, Waleed Abu al-Khair, to fifteen years in prison.[8] The article quotes the Deputy Director of the Middle East and North Africa Programme at Amnesty International as saying:

> Waleed Abu al-Khair's conviction on charges relating to national security is entirely unjustified and provides alarming evidence that the Kingdom's new anti-terrorism law is going to be used to repress peaceful political dissent.[9]

---

[4] Penal Code, art. 87bis, Order No. 66-156 of June 8, 1966, http://www.droit.mjustice.dz/legisl_nouveau/code_penal_2010/ar/index.html?i=168 (in Arabic; translated by author, I.S.) (Alg.).
[5] Penal Code, art. 218bis, Dahir 1-59-413 of 1962, http://adala.justice.gov.ma/production/legislation/ar/Nouveautes/القانون%20الجنائي.pdf (in Arabic; translated by author, I.S.) (Morocco).
[6] Law Concerning Offenses of Terrorism and its Financing art. 1(a), Royal Decree No. M/16 of 1935 Hijri, corresponding to December 27, 2013, http://boe.gov.sa/ViewSystemDetails.aspx?lang=ar&SystemID=327&VersionID=305 (in Arabic; translated by author, I.S.) (Saudi Arabia).
[7] See, e.g., Morocco: Stop Using 'Terrorism' as a Pretext to Imprison Journalists, AMNESTY INTERNATIONAL (May 20, 2014), http://www.amnesty.org/en/news/morocco-stop-using-terrorism-pretext-imprison-journalists-2014-05-20; HUMAN RIGHTS WATCH, WORLD REPORT 2009: ALGERIA (Jan. 2009), http://www.hrw.org/world-report-2009/algeria.
[8] New Anti-terror Law Used to Imprison Saudi Arabian Human Rights Activist, AMNESTY INTERNATIONAL (July 7, 2014), http://www.amnesty.org/en/news/new-anti-terror-law-used-imprison-saudi-arabian-human-rights-activist-2014-07-07.
[9] Id.

III. Special Investigative Tools

As a part of strengthening their legal measures to counter terrorism, Algeria, Morocco, and Saudi Arabia have amended their existing laws or enacted new ones to give investigators, security forces, and the courts special powers when the criminal offenses are classified as terrorist crimes. The most significant of these changes are explained below.

A. Algeria

Algeria's criminal procedure law imposes a number of restrictions on the criminal investigative process with regard to carrying out searches and time frames for detention.

Under the law, investigators are prohibited from entering personal residences without a search warrant obtained from the competent judicial authority in the geographic area where the residence is located. Furthermore, no search is allowed to take place before 5:00 a.m. or after 8:00 p.m., and the presence of the accused or his representative during the search is required.[10]

The law was amended in 1982 to lift these restrictions when the offense being investigated is classified as a terrorist act. This means that, where a terrorist crime is alleged, the search warrant does not need to be obtained from the local authority, with search warrants in relation to such offenses therefore executable anywhere in the nation and not limited to the geographic competency of the issuer;[11] a search can take place any time during day or night;[12] and the presence of the accused or his representative is not a necessity during the search.[13]

With respect to temporary detention, an accused can be taken into custody during the investigative process under certain conditions for a period not to exceed forty-eight hours; but if the crime is classified as a terrorist act this period can be extended by up to twelve days.[14]

Under Algerian law, pretrial detention is allowed under certain strict conditions and limited to a period of four months, which can be renewed twice. However, when the offense is classified as a terrorist act the pretrial detention may be renewed five times and, if the crime is transnational in nature, as many terrorist acts are, the detention period may be renewed eleven times.[15]

---

[10] Criminal Procedure Code, Order No. 155-66 of June 8, 1966, http://www.droit.mjustice.dz/portailarabe/legisl_de_06_au08/code_proc_penale_modif_ar_06.pdf (in Arabic and French) (Alg.).

[11] *Id.* art. 44.

[12] *Id.* art. 47.

[13] *Id,* art. 45.

[14] *Id.* art. 51.

[15] *Id.* art. 125bis.

B. Morocco

As of 2011, Morocco had made several amendments to its Criminal Procedure Code,[16] which included granting investigators more powers when the crime being investigated is classified as a terrorist crime. The law now includes the following:

- Investigators are authorized to seize any type of documents that may prove the commission of a crime by searching the residence of those who have possession of such documents. Normally, only the officer of the judicial police and specific other persons are allowed to see these documents before deciding whether to seize them or not. However, this restriction does not apply when the crime involved is a terrorist crime.[17]

- Normally, searches of residences cannot be conducted before 6:00 a.m. or after 9:00 p.m. When the crime being investigated is a terrorist crime these restrictions do not apply if searches during these times are considered necessary.[18]

- Investigators may detain any persons who could be helpful for the investigation for a period not to exceed forty-eight hours. In investigating terrorist crimes the period is ninety-six hours, renewable for the same period twice.[19]

- Normally, entering and searching residences for the purpose of seizing evidence requires the explicit approval of the owner of the residence. If the evidence relates to a terrorist crime and the owner abstains from giving his approval the search can be conducted following a written order of the general prosecutor.[20]

- Normally, only the investigative judge has the power to order the interception of telephonic and other means of communications. This power is now extended to the General Representative of the King when the matter relates to a terrorist crime.[21]

C. Saudi Arabia

Saudi Arabia does not have a written, comprehensive penal code but asserts that it applies Sharia' or Islamic law. In December 2001, in its first report to the Security Council Committee established pursuant to Resolution 1373 concerning counterterrorism, Saudi Arabia stipulated the following:

> In the Islamic Shariah, which the Kingdom applies and from which it derives its statutes, crimes of terrorism are included among the crimes of *hirabah*. The severest of penalties are applied to these crimes in the Islamic Shariah, as set forth in the Holy Koran [Koran

---

[16] Criminal Procedure Code, Dahir 1-58-261 of 1959, *as amended to* Oct. 27, 2011, http://adala.justice.gov.ma/production/legislation/ar/Nouveautes/الجنائية20%المسطرة20%قانون.pdf (in Arabic) (Morocco).

[17] *Id.* art. 59.

[18] *Id.* art. 62.

[19] *Id.* art. 66.

[20] *Id.* art. 79.

[21] *Id.* art. 108.

5:33]. The crimes of *hirabah* include the killing and terrorization of innocent people, spreading evil on earth (*al-ifsad fi al-ard*), theft, looting and highway robbery.[22]

In its supplementary report, submitted to the Committee in July 2002, Saudi Arabia stipulated that financing of terrorism also falls into the crime of *hirabah*:

> For its statutes, the Kingdom of Saudi Arabia relies on Islamic law. The financing of terrorism falls into the category of "spreading evil on earth" (al-ifsad fi al-ard). This may incur the non-discretionary hadd penalty for hirabah (brigandage), which can sometimes mean the application of the death penalty.[23]

In December 2013, as referred to above, Saudi Arabia enacted the Law Concerning Crimes of Terrorism and its Financing. This Law gives the Minister of Interior the power to issue arrest warrants against those suspected of having committed terrorist crimes and to delegate this power as he sees fit according to guidelines he prescribes.[24]

Investigators may arrest and detain those accused of terrorist crimes for a period or periods not to exceed six months, renewable once for another six months. Any detention beyond the renewed period must be authorized by the Specialized Criminal Court.[25] Apparently, the arrest warrants issued by the Minister of Interior are not among those subject to the supervision of the Specialized Criminal Court.

Apart from the right of the accused to inform his relatives of his arrest, investigators may prohibit any communications with the accused for a period not to exceed ninety days. Any prohibition beyond the ninety days must be referred to the Specialized Criminal Court for authorization.[26]

This new law gives the Minister of Interior judicial powers in the investigative phase of the crimes of terrorism unique among the legal systems of other countries. Among such powers are those that allow the Minister or his designee to

- Enter homes and offices at any time for the purpose of searching them and arresting persons accused of terrorist crimes;[27]

- Monitor letters, messages, publications, parcels, and other means of communication, as well as telephone conversations, and confiscate or make copies thereof whether this is in relation to a crime that has already been committed or may be committed;[28] and

---

[22] Report of the Kingdom of Saudi Arabia Submitted Pursuant to Paragraph 6 of Security Council Resolution 1373 (2001) Concerning Counter-terrorism, at 5, U.N. Doc. S/2001/1294 (Dec. 26, 2001), http://www.un.org/en/sc/ctc/resources/1373.html (scroll to Saudi Arabia).

[23] Report of the Kingdom of Saudi Arabia in Response to the Comments Contained in the Letter Dated 18 April 2002 from the Chairman of the Security Council Committee Established Pursuant to Resolution 1373 (2001) Concerning Counter-terrorism, at 4, U.N. Doc. S/2002/869 (July 10, 2002), http://www.un.org/en/sc/ctc/resources/1373.html (scroll to Saudi Arabia).

[24] Law Concerning Offenses of Terrorism and its Financing art. 4 (Saudi Arabia).

[25] *Id.* art. 5.

[26] *Id.* art. 6.

[27] *Id.* art. 16.

- Urgently order the temporary seizure for a period of three months, renewable for a similar period or periods until the investigation is complete, property suspected of having been used in terrorist crimes.[29]

The Minister of the Interior also has the discretionary power to order the release of detainees who are accused of a terrorist offense or persons convicted of such crimes during the execution of their sentences.[30]

IV. Financing of Terrorism

In accordance with the general principles of the criminal law in civil law jurisdictions, any person who assists in the commission of a crime, including by financing it, is normally considered a principal actor or participant in the crime he financed and is subject to the same penalty as those who personally commit the crime.

In Algeria, for example, article 41 of the Penal Code states that actors of a crime include those who personally commit it and those who entice them to commit it through gifts (including certainly financing) or other means of enticements.[31]

In Morocco, article 129(1) of the Penal Code states that a participant in the commission of a crime includes anyone who encourages its commission through a gift.[32] Article 130 provides that a participant in the commission of a crime must be subject to the punishment assigned to the crime.

As mentioned above, Saudi Arabia does not have a comprehensive written penal code. With regard to the existence of legal provisions aimed at suppressing the financing of terrorism, the Saudi government stated in its second letter to the UN Security Council Committee established pursuant to Resolution 1373 that the financing of terrorism falls into the category of "spreading evil on earth" (*al-ifsad fi al-ard*), which may incur the nondiscretionary *hadd* penalty for *hirabah*.[33]

However, in response to more specific requirements to combat the financing of terrorism outlined in UN Resolution 1373, and in compliance with other UN decisions, the three countries have adopted specific legal provisions.

In Algeria, the legislature made the financing of terrorism a separate crime independent from the terrorist act itself by providing in article 87bis(4) of the Penal Code that anyone who praises, encourages, or finances by any means acts of terrorism must be punished by five to ten years imprisonment and a fine of 100,000 to 500,000 Algerian dinars.[34]

---

[28] *Id.* art. 17.
[29] *Id.* art. 18.
[30] *Id.* art. 24.
[31] Penal Code art. 41 (Alg.).
[32] Penal Code art. 129(1) (Morocco).
[33] U.N. Doc. S/2002/869, *supra* note 23, at 5.
[34] Penal Code art. 87bis (4) (Alg.).

In addition, in 2005, Algeria enacted a special law to prevent money laundering and financing of terrorism, which makes all suspicious financial transactions subject to scrutiny.[35] Article 15 of this law requires that basically all financial and some other institutions refer to a special investigative unit, in the manner prescribed, any transactions suspected of involving the crime of financing of terrorism. If the special investigative unit finds reasons to believe that a crime was committed then it must refer its findings to the competent criminal legal authority.[36]

In 2011, Morocco added article 218(4) to its Penal Code, which makes the financing of terrorism a crime even if the act of terrorism itself did not take place. It stipulates that the following must be considered terrorist acts:

> The carrying out by any means, directly or indirectly, the offering, collection, or arranging the obtaining of funds, properties, or anything of value for the purpose of using them or with the knowledge that they will be used in full or in part to commit a terrorist act whether such act takes place or not.[37]

Morocco also has an anti-money-laundering law[38] and a special administrative unit[39] to monitor financial transactions that might involve money laundering or terrorism financing. This unit follows the global standard set up by the Financial Action Task Force (FATF) for anti-money laundering and combating the financing of terrorism (AML/CFT). One of the major tasks of this unit, pursuant to article 18 of the law, is to refer to the competent judicial authorities for investigation and prosecution any financial transactions suspected of being related to the financing of terrorism.

In Saudi Arabia, article 1(a) of the 2013 Law Concerning Offenses of Terrorism and its Financing[40] adopts for the offense of financing of terrorism the same definition adopted by the International Convention for the Suppression of the Financing of Terrorism.[41]

Saudi Arabia also enacted an Anti-Money Laundering Law in April 2012, and issued its implementing instructions.[42] Pursuant to article 9 of this Law any suspicious financial transactions involving the financing of terrorism has to be referred to the special investigative

---

[35] Law on the Prevention and Control of Money Laundering and Terrorist Financing, Law No. 05-01of 1425 Hijri, corresponding to 2005, http://www.droit mjustice.dz/loi_prevent_lutte_blanchim_argent_financem_terrorisme.pdf (in Arabic and French) (Algeria).

[36] *Id.* art. 16.

[37] Penal Code art. 218(4) (Morocco).

[38] Anti-Money-Laundering Law, Dahir 1-07-79 of 2007, http://www.marocdroit.com/-الأموال-غسل-بمكافحة-المتعلق-القانون a64.html بالمغرب (in Arabic) (Morocco).

[39] This unit was created pursuant to article 14 of the Anti-Money-Laundering Law by Ministerial Decree No. 2-08-572 of 2008, BULLETIN OFFICIEL No. 5700 of Dec. 24, 2009.

[40] Law Concerning Offenses of Terrorism and its Financing art. 1(a) (Saudi Arabia).

[41] International Convention for the Suppression of the Financing of Terrorism, Dec. 9, 1999, 2178 U.N.T.S. 197, https://treaties.un.org/doc/db/Terrorism/english-18-11.pdf.

[42] Anti-Money Laundering Law, Royal Decree M31 of 5/11/1433 Hijri, corresponding to Apr. 3, 2012 (Saudi Arabia). Both the Law and its Implementing Instructions are available on the website of the Saudi Arabia Anti-Money Laundering Committee, *at* http://www.sama.gov.sa/MoneyLaundry/DocLib1/ غسل مكافحة لنظام التنفيذية اللائحة الأموال.pdf (in Arabic). An English translation of the Law is available on the same site, *at* http://www.sama.gov.sa/sites/samaen/RulesRegulation/BankingSystem/Pages/anti_money_laundering_%28aml%29_law_ar_en.pdf.

unit, which will decide if there is enough evidence to refer the matter to the competent criminal authority.

V. Religious Element of Terrorism

Arguably, an effective counterterrorism policy also seeks to address the religious motivational element involved in acts of terrorism. The prohibitions of the criminal justice system do not necessarily change in the mind of potential terrorists what they believe is a divine command calling on them to fight the nonbelievers, meaning non-Muslims. Morocco and Saudi Arabia have apparently realized the importance of dealing with this religious element of terrorism by means other than the criminal justice system.

In its supplementary report of October 13, 2004, Morocco informed the United Nations Counter-Terrorism Committee of the acceleration of in-depth educational, religious, and cultural reforms as part of its counterterrorism strategy, asserting that

> [m]ajor reforms have been carried out with respect to religious activity, in an effort to protect Morocco from any stirrings of extremism and terrorism.[43]

Similarly, in a paper dated November 2012, Saudi Arabia outlined three prongs of policy to counter terrorism.[44] One of these prongs is concerned with changing the mindset of potential terrorists to overcome extremism, described as follows in the paper:

> This approach constitutes a "war of ideas," which aims to instill the concepts of moderation and tolerance, and to undermine any justifications for extremism and terrorism on an intellectual level.[45]

The Saudi Government appears to identify religious schools and religious teaching as a source of extremism by stating that this approach extends "to Saudi religious schools" and that

> Imams have been prohibited from incitement and talk of intolerance, and the Ministry of Islamic Affairs is conducting a program to educate imams and monitor mosques and religious education to purge extremism and intolerance.[46]

It is possible that such measures in both Morocco and Saudi Arabia could be more effective in changing minds and beliefs than the prohibitions contained in the criminal laws. However, no specific information was located about the substance or content of these measures and programs intended to instill moderation and tolerance among extremists or potential terrorists.

---

[43] Supplementary Report of the Kingdom of Morocco to the Security Council Committee Established Pursuant to Resolution 1373 (2001), at 5, U.N. Doc. S/2004/826 (Oct. 13, 2004), http://www.un.org/en/sc/ctc/resources/1373.html (scroll to Morocco).

[44] THE KINGDOM OF SAUDI ARABIA, INITIATIVES AND ACTIONS TO COMBAT TERRORISM (Nov. 2012), available on the website of the Saudi Arabian Embassy in Washington, DC, at http://www.saudiembassy.net/files/PDF/Reports/Counterterrorism.pdf.

[45] Id. at 5.

[46] Id.

VI. Non-legal Response to Terrorism

Arguably, an effective counterterrorism policy also seeks to address the religious motivational element involved in acts of terrorism. The prohibitions of the criminal justice system do not necessarily change in the mind of potential terrorists what they believe is a divine command calling on them to fight the nonbelievers, meaning non-Muslims. Morocco and Saudi Arabia have apparently realized the importance of dealing with this religious element of terrorism.

For several years the governments of Saudi Arabia, Morocco, and Algeria have been adopting policies designed to prevent and protect against the threat of terrorism other than through the legal system per se. These policies focus on enhancing the capabilities of security forces and on trying to deal with certain religious ideas that play a role in formulating the mindset of terrorists.

A. Saudi Arabia

In a 2012 report explaining its policies in this regard, the Government of the Kingdom of Saudi Arabia points to the following programs and actions taken to enhance the performance of its security agencies in matters related to terrorism:[47]

1. Restructuring the operations of the Ministry of Interior, under whose authority the security forces operate, in order to prevent terrorist attacks and better address the dismantling of the "physical presence of Al-Qaeda" in the Kingdom;[48]

2. Maintaining rigorous standards for the security forces through continuing training and participation in joint programs throughout the world, "including in Europe and the United States";[49]

3. Conducting joint missions and exchanging information;[50]

4. Deployment of new technologies to complement the "sophistication of Saudi Arabia's human resources";[51] and

5. Engaging neighborhood community members to work directly with the police and encouraging them to provide "tips and leads about suspicious activity."[52]

With respect to the activities targeted at addressing the religious element of terrorism, the Saudi Government has adopted what it calls "soft" counterterrorism policies. In explaining this approach the report states the following:

---

[47] THE KINGDOM OF SAUDI ARABIA, INITIATIVES AND ACTIONS TO COMBAT TERRORISM (Nov. 2012), http://www.saudiembassy.net/files/PDF/Reports/Counterterrorism.pdf.

[48] *Id.* at 3.

[49] *Id.*

[50] *Id.*

[51] *Id.*

[52] *Id.*

> This approach constitutes a "war of ideas," which aims to instill the concepts of moderation and tolerance, and to undermine any justifications for extremism and terrorism on an intellectual level. In doing so, Saudi Arabia is protecting vulnerable groups, such as youth, and any potentially disenfranchised elements of society.[53]

The Government points to a number of initiatives implemented in this regard, including a "public awareness campaign," "public and religious education," "counter-radicalization program," and "rehabilitation program." In explaining the framework of these programs, the Government was candid in acknowledging the role of religious functionaries in cultivating an atmosphere of intolerance and extremism by stipulating that, through these programs,

> Imams have been prohibited from incitement and talk of intolerance, and the Ministry of Islamic Affairs is conducting a program to educate imams and monitor mosques and religious education to purge extremism and intolerance.[54]

We note, however, that the Government faces various challenges in this area as the religious establishment in Saudi Arabia preaches a version of Islam that does not tolerate others. For example, the official teaching considers attending a Christian celebration or festivity a "sin and transgression"[55] and describes the Sufis, who are a part of the Muslim community pursuant to the teaching of all traditional schools of Islamic thought, as a "misguided group" with whom "it is not permissible to keep company" or "befriend them."[56]

According to a lengthy, two-part report published on a website under the auspices of the Saudi Ministry of Islamic Affairs and attributed to a spokesman of the Saudi Ministry of Interior, the number of detainees for terrorist crimes as of April 2013, had reached 2,772 persons, who have been referred to the competent judicial authorities.[57] Another report, published on the website of the Saudi Ministry of Foreign Affairs, contains general political statements such as "the Kingdom has responded to the acts of violence and terrorism locally and internationally by fighting them locally and denouncing them internationally and proving to the whole world its seriousness in countering terrorism."[58] However, neither report describes judicial policies regarding terrorism cases or the approach to implementing legal and non-legal responses to terrorism.

---

[53] *Id.* at 5.

[54] *Id.* at 6.

[55] *Ruling on Attending Festivities of Christians*, GENERAL PRESIDENCY OF SCHOLARLY RESEARCH AND IFTA', http://www.alifta.net/Fatawa/FatawaDetails.aspx?languagename=en&View=Page&PageID=513&PageNo=1&BookID=7 (last visited Feb. 23, 2015).

[56] *Sufism*, GENERAL PRESIDENCY OF SCHOLARLY RESEARCH AND IFTA', http://www.alifta.net/Fatawa/FatawaChapters.aspx?languagename=en&View=Page&PageID=14&PageNo=1&BookID=24 (last visited Feb. 23, 2015).

[57] TRIAL OF THE DEVIANT GROUP IN SAUDI ARABIA, 1ST PART (Apr. 1, 2013), http://www.assakina.com/news/23389.html *and* 2ND PART (Feb. 25, 2015), http://www.assakina.com/news/64284.html (in Arabic).

[58] *The Strategy of the Kingdom in Fighting Terrorism Locally, Regionally, and Internationally*, MINISTRY OF FOREIGN AFFAIRS, http://www.mofa.gov.sa/ServicesAndInformation/news/GovernmentNews/Pages/g9r.aspx (last updated Oct. 9, 2013) (in Arabic).

B. Morocco

In its *2013 Country Reports on Terrorism*, the US Department of State stated that Morocco has "a comprehensive counterterrorism strategy that includes vigilant security measures, regional and international cooperation, and counter-radicalization policies."[59] The report indicated that Morocco pursues various programs aimed at improving the performance of its security forces in combating terrorism, including the following:

1. Participation in the Department of State's Antiterrorism Assistance (ATA) program, which provided the Moroccan Department of National Security (DGSN) and the Royal Gendarmerie with training in cyberforensics, crime-scene forensics, and executive leadership;

2. Participation in Global Counterterrorism Forum (GCTF) and US Department of Justice programs to improve technical investigative training for police and prosecutors;

3. Participation in a number of multilateral training and operation exercises, which according to the State Department "have enhanced border security and improved capabilities to counter illicit traffic and terrorism"; and

4. Counterterrorism actions taken by the Moroccan security forces, which appear to have been successful to the extent that Morocco seeks to play a prominent role, with the blessing of the State Department, in the training of its neighbors in North and West Africa.

According to a news article dated March 2015, the Moroccan government has announced the creation of a "Central Bureau of Judicial Investigation" whose objective is to confront security challenges, including terrorism.[60] The same report states that the number of criminal cases classified as terrorism cases in Morocco in 2014 was 147, up from 64 in 2013. These cases involved 323 people in 2014, compared to 138 in 2013.

Previously, a news report in October 2014 stated that the Moroccan Minister of Interior had disclosed a new security program intended, in its first phase, to protect the strategic facilities in six major cities: Rabat, Casablanca, Marrakech, Fez, Tangier, and Agadir.[61] The article also mentions that Morocco had officially announced that it provided the United Arab Emirates (UAE) with military aid to help them confront what it called "terrorist threats," and quoted the Moroccan Foreign Minister as explaining that the aid comes within the framework of the bilateral relationship, but that Morocco would be ready to extend its aid to other countries in the region "concerned with terrorist threats."[62]

---

[59] U.S. DEPARTMENT OF STATE, COUNTRY REPORTS ON TERRORISM 2013: MIDDLE EAST AND NORTH AFRICA, ch. 2 (Apr. 2014), http://www.state.gov/j/ct/rls/crt/2013/224823.htm.

[60] *Morocco Creates an Internal Intelligence Agency to Combat Terrorism*, ROAYAH NEWS (Mar. 22, 2015), http://www.roayahnews.com/830931-22/المغرب-ينشئ-وكالة-استخبارات-داخلية-لم.html.

[61] *"Warned" Moroccan Security Program to Combat Terrorism*, AL JAZEERA (Oct. 30, 2014), http://www.aljazeera.net/news/reportsandinterviews/2014/10/29/حذر-برنامج-أمني-مغربي-لمكافحة-الإرهاب.

[62] *Id.*

Morocco has also adopted a "soft" counterterrorism policy but that policy differs from Saudi Arabia's in two respects. The first difference is its emphasis on educating and finding employment for youth and on helping other disadvantaged sections of society, such as through expanding the legal rights of women.[63] The second is its emphasis on teaching adherence to the precepts of Islam as developed by the Maliki School of Islamic thought. In this respect the Government of Morocco perceives the "violent Islamist extremist ideologies" to be imported into the country from abroad because such ideologies are not supported by the mainstream Maliki School of Sunni Islam.[64]

In a report prepared in 2013 by the CNA Corporation, a nonprofit research organization that operates the Center for Naval Analyses and the Institute for Public Research, the authors refer to Morocco's approach to countering terrorism, which includes utilizing law enforcement and intelligence gathering procedures as well as "soft power" programs and initiatives related to religious education and discussions with youth about the true meaning of religion. The authors of the report state that, "[b]y providing healthcare and job training to the poor, expanding rural infrastructure, and improving the overall livelihood of Moroccans, the Moroccan government hopes to counter the appeal of extremist messages and ideologies, especially among the poor and disadvantaged."[65] Furthermore, "[t]he Moroccan government also considers political reforms and increased attention to human rights issues as additional components of its efforts to combat the root causes of terrorism."[66]

In terms of reinforcing the influence of the Maliki School, initiatives include "upgrading places of worship, closing unregulated mosques, rehabilitating those who have been convicted of a terror-related crime, promoting Moroccan religious values on television and radio, and modernizing the teaching of Islam."[67] The report lists the following examples:

- The development of "a curriculum for Morocco's imams for countering violent extremism and advancing tolerance";

- The establishment of the Moroccan Council of Ulama for Europe and the Minister Delegate for Moroccans Living Abroad, aimed at promoting religious tolerance among Moroccans living in Europe;

- A new Islamic satellite television channel, launched by the King of Morocco, which advocates Islamic ideals of tolerance, taking direct aim at jihadist clerics and their media."[68]

---

[63] *Id.*

[64] *Id.*

[65] ERIC V. THOMPSON & WILL MCCANTS, PARTNERS AGAINST TERROR: OPPORTUNITIES AND CHALLENGES FOR U.S.-MOROCCAN COUNTERTERRORISM COOPERATION 3 (2013), http://www.cna.org/sites/default/files/research/PartnersAgainstTerrorism2.pdf.

[66] *Id.*

[67] *Id.*

[68] *Id.* at 4.

C. Algeria

Algeria has made consistent efforts to enhance the capabilities of its security forces. According to the Department of State's *2013 Country Reports on Terrorism*, "the Government of Algeria has multiple law enforcement, intelligence, and security agencies with delineated responsibilities to address counterterrorism, counter-intelligence, media monitoring, investigations, border security, crisis response, and anti-corruption."[69] The report identifies the following initiatives in Algeria:

1. Working toward building the capacity of the National Institute of Forensic Science and Criminology in order to obtain certification from the International Organization for Standardization (this Institute belongs to the National Gendarmerie, one of the Algerian security agencies);

2. Obtaining the US Federal Bureau of Investigation's Combined DNA Index System (CODIS),[70] which allows Algeria to share DNA data with other foreign security forces in their joint fight against terrorism; and

3. Consulting with the US Department of Justice's International Criminal Investigative Training Assistance Program on targeted capacity-building and training in forensics, criminal investigation, and border security.

A media report dated December 2014 indicated that the Criminal Court in Algiers will, during 2015, address twenty-seven cases related to terrorism. Among the most prominent of these cases is that involving friends and family members of convicted terrorist Abd al-Hamid abu Zaid. The accused are charged with belonging to an armed terrorist group, compromising the security of citizens, incitement of terrorist acts, and financing an armed terrorist group.[71]

Recently, the Criminal Court in Algiers began the trial of forty-one terrorists headed by Abdelmalek Droukdel, the leader of the terrorist group known as al-Qaeda in the Islamic Maghreb, who are facing charges related to several murders committed during the 1990s in Algiers and in Boumerdes.[72]

Algeria's approach to dealing with the religious element of terrorism differs from both Saudi Arabia and Morocco. The Algerian government does not allow anyone to preach in mosques other than those appointed by the government to do so.[73] This lessens the possibility of importing "violent Islamist extremist ideologies," gives the government the capability of

---

[69] *Id.*

[70] *Id.*

[71] *Supplementary List by the Felony [Court] in the Capital: 140 Cases Ready for Trial, 27 of which Are for Terrorism*, RADIO ALGERIE (Dec. 14, 2014), http://www.radioalgerie.dz/news/ar/article/20141214/22621.html.

[72] *Algiers: Trial of 41 Terrorists Including the Commander of al-Qaeda in the Islamic Maghreb, Abdelmalek Droukdel*, ALCHOUROUK.COM (Feb. 15, 2015), http://www.alchourouk.com/93692/691/1/-الجزائر: محاكمة 41 ارهابيا منهم أمير تنظيم القاعدة في بلاد المغرب الاسلامي عبد المالك دروكدال - html.

[73] *Id.*

monitoring mosques "for possible security-related offenses," and "prohibits the use of mosques as public meeting places outside of regular prayer hours."[74]

In a 2012 report on counterterrorism strategies in Algeria, Indonesia, and Saudi Arabia, the authors state that "Algeria does not have a comprehensive approach to counter-terrorism and the underlying strategy is not entirely known."[75] At the same time the report opines that "it can be argued that Algeria is moving towards a more holistic approach to tackling recruitment by jihadi Salafists and terrorism, and it is currently combining a 'hard' (military) approach to combat armed cells with a 'soft' (religious) approach to prevent religiously motivated recruits from engaging in terrorism."[76] However, the report goes on to express the view that "the Algerian regime is preoccupied with its survival and sustaining its power structure, and that this attitude dictates Algeria's counterterrorism effort."[77] The report adds that "counter-terrorism measures are designed … to ensure the people's loyalty to the state" and that, "[h]istorically, civil society and associational life have been severely suppressed, with the exception of the brief period between 1988 and 1992."[78]

Final Note

We note that, while the Saudi Government is fighting terrorist organizations within the Kingdom, some reports suggest it is actually supporting similar groups (such as al-Nusra) who are fighting abroad. In a speech delivered at Harvard University in 2014, the US Vice President reportedly acknowledged that Saudi Arabia, among other countries, was too focused on opposing Syrian leader Bashar al-Assad to see the potential trouble being created by arming and financing radical extremists.[79]

We also note that the press has recently published what appears to be a Moroccan government top-secret document showing Morocco's collusion with groups carrying out terrorist actions in a foreign country.[80]

---

[74] *Id.*

[75] NOORHAIDI HASAN ET AL., COUNTER-TERRORISM STRATEGIES IN INDONESIA, ALGERIA AND SAUDI ARABIA 94 (2012), http://english.wodc.nl/images/1806-volledige-tekst_tcm45-435986.pdf.

[76] *Id.*

[77] *Id.* at 71.

[78] *Id.*

[79] *All Politics is Personal; VP Biden Delivers Address at Kennedy School Forum*, HARVARD KENNEDY SCHOOL (Oct. 3, 2014), http://www.hks.harvard.edu/news-events/news/articles/joe-biden-forum-event.

[80] *"Death Deal" Between Moroccan Intelligence and "Droukdel" in a Secret Meeting in Mauritania*, WESTERN SAHARA NEWS, http://diasporasaharaui-en.blogspot.com/2015/02/death-deal-between-moroccan.html (last visited Apr. 13, 2015).